EXTREME CAREERS™

BOMB SQUAD EXPERTS

Life Defusing Explosive Devices

Suzanne J. Murdico

rosen
central™

The Rosen Publishing Group, Inc., New York

For Vinnie

Published in 2004 by The Rosen Publishing Group, Inc.
29 East 21st Street, New York, NY 10010

Library of Congress Cataloging-in-Publication Data

Murdico, Suzanne J.
Bomb squad experts: life defusing explosive devices / by Suzanne J. Murdico.— 1st ed.
    p. cm. — (Extreme careers)
Summary: Examines the careers available in the field of explosive detection/defusing, discussing the necessary education, training, and on-the-job duties.
Includes bibliographical references and index.
ISBN 0-8239-3968-5 (lib. bdg.)
1. Bombing investigation—Juvenile literature. 2. Bomb threats—Juvenile literature. 3. Bomb reconnaissance—Juvenile literature. 4. Ordnance disposal units—Juvenile literature. [1. Bomb reconnaissance—Vocational guidance. 2. Bombing investigation—Vocational guidance. 3. Vocational guidance.] I. Title. II. Series.
HV8079.B62M87 2003
363.25'964—dc21

2002153684

Manufactured in the United States of America

Contents

Introduction: An Explosive Situation

Terrorists have hidden an explosive device somewhere deep within a city skyscraper. The clock on the device ticks down the remaining few minutes before the bomb is set to detonate. If the bomb explodes, it will take down the building and many of the people inside.

Several bomb squad experts race into the building. Tension mounts as they scramble to locate the ticking device. Finally, one bomb technician finds the explosive. But now only thirty seconds remain on the clock before certain death and destruction.

A rainbow of brightly colored wires protrudes from the device. With sweat dripping from his brow, the bomb tech must make a life-or-death decision in the

Members of the bomb squad have to act fast to defuse potentially fatal situations. This image is from the film *Blown Away*, which tells the story of a bomb squad expert, played by actor Jeff Bridges *(left)*.

blink of an eye. Which wire should he cut? Red? Green? Blue?

Five . . . four . . . three . . . Now with the clock reading just two seconds before detonation, the bomb tech makes his best guess. He holds his breath, reaches forward with wire cutters, and snips the red wire. With only one second remaining on the clock, the room suddenly becomes silent. The device has stopped ticking! The bomb technician breathes a sigh of relief. There will be no explosion. The bomb squad has saved the day.

The Real Story

The previous scenario might make an exciting scene in an action film. But it isn't an entirely accurate depiction of how bomb squad experts really work. Bomb technicians do face extremely dangerous situations on a daily basis. With every bomb threat, they put their lives at risk to ensure the public's safety.

There are many differences, though, between Hollywood's version of bomb squad work and the real thing. For one, bomb technicians rarely rely on luck or guesswork when dealing with explosives. Bomb techs are highly trained and constantly work on sharpening their skills. They study how bombs are made and stay current on the latest technology used by bomb makers. When a bomb tech disarms an explosive device, he or she knows exactly what to do. There is no last-minute guessing as to which wire should be cut.

Another difference is that real bomb techs try not to take a hands-on approach when disarming explosives. Safety is their primary concern. Bomb squad experts know that the farther away they are from an explosive device, the safer they are. So whenever possible, they rely on X-ray cameras, robots, and other high-tech tools to help them do their work.

Bomb Squad Work

Bomb squad experts are responsible for the detecting, disarming, and disposing of bombs. Members of the bomb squad generally don't refer to these devices as bombs, though. They usually refer to any suspicious-looking objects as "packages." For safety reasons, bomb techs consider all packages to be extremely dangerous until they are proven not to be or until they are disarmed.

Another responsibility of the bomb squad is to help ensure the safety of politicians, dignitaries, and other VIPs (very important persons). Because VIPs are common targets for terrorists trying to make political statements, safety is a primary concern. Before VIP gatherings, bomb techs conduct security searches. They check every square inch from floor to ceiling to make certain that no explosive devices are present. The same type of thorough searching is also performed before special events, such as the Olympics or the Super Bowl, are held.

In the unfortunate event that an explosion does occur, the bomb tech's role is to help in the investigation. The goal is to determine who is responsible for the bombing. Bomb techs work closely with law enforcement officers to inspect the bomb site for clues. Bomb squad experts may also help bring criminals to justice by testifying in court cases.

Explosive Forces

Bomb techs learn early in their training that the size of a package is not an accurate indication of a bomb's explosive force. They must exercise the same amount of caution when dealing with a package the size of a tennis ball as they would with a refrigerator-sized package. It's possible that even a small bomb can be powerful enough to demolish an entire building.

The explosive force of a bomb depends on the materials used to make it. In any case, though, it's always very dangerous and often unpredictable. When a bomb explodes, it sends blast fragments flying through the air at high speeds. Some bombers even go a step further by adding shrapnel, such as nails or marbles, to an explosive device. The shrapnel is intended to cause even more injuries and deaths than the bomb alone.

Bomb squad experts in Atlanta, Georgia, released this photo of representative items that were used in a nightclub bombing in that city in February 1997.

1/4-Inch-Thick Steel Plates

Plastic Containers

Duct Tape

Dynamite

Green Backpack

Electrical Tape

6-Volt Lantern Batteries

Alarm Clocks

6 Dozen Wire Nails

Some bombs do more than send out blast fragments. High explosives send out shock waves or blast waves, which are very powerful bursts of air that travel at high speeds. These shock waves are so powerful, in fact, that they can smash cars, demolish buildings, and kill people. Shock waves start at the site of the blast and spread outward. The impact is strongest at that central point and gradually weakens as the shock waves extend outward.

Hoaxes and Booby Traps

In addition to the dangers associated with explosives, bomb techs must deal with specific threats against their own lives. Hoaxes and booby traps are devices designed by bombers especially to hurt or kill bomb techs or other law enforcement officers.

A hoax might occur when a bomber plants two bombs near each other. One of these bombs may be a fake or a small bomb without much explosive power. The bomber might put the fake bomb in plain view or detonate the small bomb. This draws attention to the first bomb and brings bomb techs to the area to investigate. With attention focused on the hoax device, the bomber then detonates the real bomb.

Bomb techs must also be aware that the area surrounding a bomb or suspicious-looking package may be booby-trapped. For example, doors or drawers may be rigged to explode when opened. A nearly invisible wire, called a trip wire, may be stretched across the threshold of a door. When an unsuspecting person tries to enter the building, the trip wire triggers an explosion. Bomb techs learn to be wary of any objects found at bomb scenes. Even an innocent-looking flashlight may be booby-trapped.

Reasons for Bombings

After learning about the extreme dangers of explosive devices, you may be wondering why anyone would make and plant a bomb. The reasons behind bombings are probably as unique as the bombers themselves. Bombers may be fired employees or jealous lovers seeking revenge, members of organized crime or rival gangs, or people playing pranks or looking for thrills.

Bombers often use explosions to terrorize people. Pictured here is the immediate aftermath of the bombing of an abortion clinic in Atlanta, Georgia, in January 1997. Flying debris rains down on emergency vehicles.

In recent years, terrorism has become a more common reason for bombings. Terrorists use violence to threaten, hurt, or kill people and to destroy property. They may disapprove of the government and use bombs as a means of drawing attention to their political beliefs or goals. For some terrorists, religious or moral beliefs motivate their actions. Places of worship and abortion clinics may be the targets of these bombers.

Regardless of their reasons, bombers are definitely more active today than in years past. Since the terrorist attacks of September 11, 2001, there has been a noticeable increase in bomb scares in the United States. In New York City alone, the bomb squad may deal with as many as fifty suspicious-looking packages every day. But for bomb squad experts, it's business as usual.

Detecting Bombs

1

When a suspicious-looking package is found, the bomb squad is often called to the scene. The object might be anything—a sealed cardboard box, an ice chest, or a suitcase that has been left unattended or placed in an unusual location. Although most of these items turn out to be harmless, some may in fact contain explosive devices.

Bomb technicians don't have the luxury of making guesses or taking chances. They must assume that any suspicious object may be a bomb and therefore is a potential threat to public safety. Bomb techs also take all bomb threats very seriously—from a scribbled note on the bathroom wall at a school to a lengthy letter written by a known terrorist.

At the Scene

Regular police officers are usually the first to arrive at the scene of a suspicious object or a bomb threat. They clear the building or area and cordon it off with crime scene tape. All necessary precautions are taken to protect the public.

Although some bombs are left in plain sight, others are very well hidden. With bomb threats, the location of the bomb (if there actually is one) is often

The first order of business in a bomb threat is safety. Police keep spectators and the media well back from any dangerous area. Police then wait for the bomb techs to investigate.

unknown. In these instances, the first step for the bomb squad is to find the explosives. For this step, bomb technicians may receive assistance from some nonhuman members of the bomb squad.

Bomb Dogs

Dogs are more than just man's best friend. For bomb technicians, dogs are essential members of the bomb squad team. Bomb dogs, as they are often called, are sent into areas where bomb threats exist. These areas might include airports, office buildings, or parking garages.

The bomb dog's job is to use its excellent sense of smell to find explosive devices. The dog then alerts its handler—a police detective or bomb technician—of the bomb's location. Bomb dogs work very closely with their handlers. In fact, they usually live with the handlers as members of their families.

Types of Bomb Dogs

The two breeds of dogs most often used by bomb squads are Labrador retrievers and German shepherds.

Bomb-sniffing dogs, like this German shepherd sniffing packages at an airport, are essential to bomb detection. A dog's keen sense of smell can detect explosive materials through containers.

These dogs are ideally suited for explosives detection work. They are very intelligent, are easily trained, and have an especially keen sense of smell.

For these reasons, Labrador retrievers and German shepherds are also used as guide dogs for people who are visually impaired or physically disabled. Not all dogs excel at the special demands of guide dog training, however. For example, some dogs may be too friendly, while others may become startled too easily. Often, however, these dogs can be retrained to become excellent bomb dogs.

Bomb Dog Training

Dogs on the bomb squad are trained strictly on a praise and reward system. First, handlers hide fake explosives in a variety of places—in a car trunk, in a suitcase, in a desk drawer. When a dog locates the explosives, it is praised and rewarded with food. This way, the dog associates finding a bomb with being rewarded, and it is encouraged to repeat this process.

Bomb dogs are trained to sniff out many different scents associated with explosives. When they locate

Bomb-Sniffing Bees

Can you imagine ordinary honeybees as the next step in the evolution of explosives detection? The idea may not be as far-fetched as you might think. Scientists at the Pentagon are training bees to sniff out tiny traces of explosives that might otherwise have gone undetected.

Bees are extremely sensitive to odors. In fact, experts feel that bees may be even more sensitive to smells than dogs. In tests performed by the U.S. Air Force, bees located chemicals used in explosives nearly 100 percent of the time.

The method for training bees to find explosives is similar to that used for training dogs. Rather than dog food, though, the bees are rewarded with sugar water when they locate a certain scent. The cue to search for a new scent must be taught to just one bee. Amazingly, that bee then alerts the rest of the hive to switch from flower sniffing to bomb sniffing.

As you might guess, bomb-sniffing bees are not quite as versatile as bomb-sniffing dogs. After all, it wouldn't be practical to let a swarm of bees loose around the general public. But, in the future, bees may serve an important function in the field of bomb detection.

the scent, the dogs are taught to alert their handlers by sitting down or by pawing or scratching the ground. Each handler understands his or her dog's particular signal and knows that the dog has discovered an explosive. One thing that bomb dogs are taught never to do is to bite, shake, or paw at a suspect package. This type of motion could easily detonate a bomb, injuring or killing the dog as well as people in the area.

To become a bomb squad member, a dog must graduate from a certified training program that usually lasts for several months. The training doesn't end there, though. Bomb dogs continue to train for several hours every day so that their skills stay sharp and they're ready to locate the real explosives.

X-ray Cameras

Another important tool in bomb detection is the X-ray camera. Similar to X-ray machines used to see inside the human body, bomb squad X-ray cameras are used to see inside suspicious packages. Unlike most medical versions, though, X-ray cameras used by bomb technicians are small and portable.

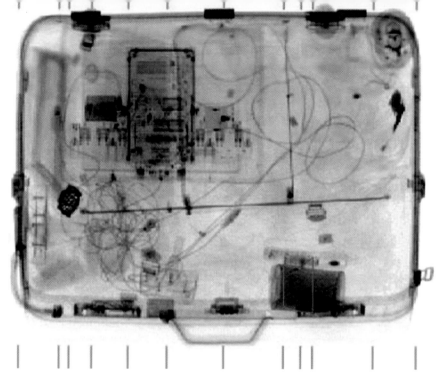

X-ray machines used at airports are similar to the X-ray machines used in hospitals. This machine, the CTX 5000 explosives detection system, was first used during the 1996 Olympic Games in Atlanta, Georgia. The red lines indicate the presence of a bomb.

Bomb techs carry these X-ray cameras with them on the job. Without having to touch a package, they can take an X ray of it. Even if it turns out to be a false alarm, the bomb techs don't have to take unnecessary risks. But if the suspicious package does turn out to be an explosive device, the bomb techs must now perform the most dangerous part of their job. They must disarm and dispose of a live bomb.

Bomb Disarming and Disposal

2

In order to safely disarm and dispose of explosives, the bomb squad must be familiar with a wide range of devices. The technology is constantly changing, so bomb techs must stay up-to-date. Some of the explosives they may encounter include the following:

- Military explosives are devices normally used by the armed forces for combat training and in times of war. Bombers sometimes buy and use stolen military explosives, such as hand grenades and missiles.

- Homemade bombs are explosive devices created from fairly easy-to-find components. Some of these components can be obtained from electronics stores, while others are sold at sporting goods stores.

Homemade bombs are often so unstable, though, that they end up injuring or killing the bomb maker before they reach their intended target.

• Dirty bombs, also known as improvised radiation-dispersal devices, are one of the newest and most dangerous types of explosives. Dirty bombs are homemade nuclear devices, which are intended to spread radioactive contamination and kill thousands of people.

Members of the U.S. Army's 731st Explosive Ordnance Disposal Company set explosives to destroy Taliban rockets and mortar shells in Kandahar, Afghanistan, after the U.S. invasion in late 2001. The inset shows a homemade time bomb made out of a canteen.

After the bomb squad has established what type of explosive device they are dealing with, they must make a crucial decision. The bomb techs must determine the best way to disarm the device, or make it inactive. This step is critical because one false move could mean the difference between life and death—not only for the bomb squad but also for other people in the area.

The bomb squad uses three main techniques for disarming and disposing of explosives—defusing, containing, and detonating. The decision about which method to use depends on several factors, including the type of explosive device and its location. And sometimes a combination of methods is used.

Defusing

When an explosive device is located in a populated area, the bomb squad doesn't have a lot of options for disarming it. In general, it is too risky to move the device to a more isolated area. So the bomb techs must defuse it on the spot.

Defusing bombs is tricky business. Each bomb is different because of the person who created it and the types of materials he or she used. Bomb techs must examine an explosive device and determine how it works and how it can be disarmed—all within a matter of minutes or even seconds.

Robotic Help

Most bomb squads have at least one robot that can provide assistance after a bomb has been located. Because the robots can be operated by remote control, bomb techs are able to stay at a safe distance from the explosives. The robots have wheels or tracks

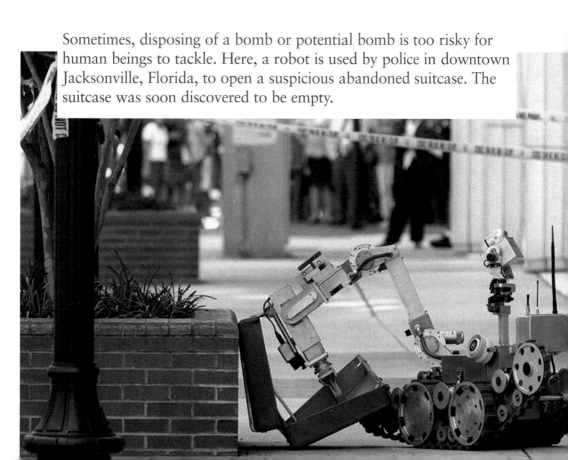

Sometimes, disposing of a bomb or potential bomb is too risky for human beings to tackle. Here, a robot is used by police in downtown Jacksonville, Florida, to open a suspicious abandoned suitcase. The suitcase was soon discovered to be empty.

that allow movement over most types of terrain, including stairways. They all have a movable arm that has the ability to grip things. This arm can perform a variety of tasks, such as unlocking doors, lifting objects, and operating an X-ray camera.

In some circumstances, the bomb squad may use a robot to actually disarm an explosive. One commonly used method is to have the robot fire a disrupter cannon. This device shoots a stream of water at speeds of up to 800 miles per hour. The disrupter's powerful force shatters the internal elements of the bomb before it has a chance to explode.

Although robots are the first choice for disarming bombs, they can't be used in every situation. For example, a bomb may be located in a small space where a robot can't reach it. In these cases, a bomb squad expert must bravely approach the explosive device and disarm it by hand. This means separating the detonator from the explosives.

Suiting Up

Before bomb techs get close to an explosive device, they put on safety gear—and plenty of it! The main

Putting on and moving around in a bomb suit can be cumbersome. It's also the best protection a human can have if he or she must approach a bomb.

safety gear is a bomb suit that provides head-to-toe coverage. (The only body parts that stay uncovered are the hands, because the fingers must remain unrestricted.)

The bomb suit is made of several layers of Kevlar—the same high-tech material used to make the bulletproof vests worn by police officers. The bomb suit is huge, weighing between 80 and 100 pounds. It's so large and awkward that bomb techs must help each other climb into it. And, as you might expect from something so big and heavy, the bomb suit is very hot. It's so hot, in fact, that the helmet comes equipped with a blower to keep the face shield from steaming up!

Wearing the bulky suit may make bomb techs look like they're preparing for a moon walk. The suit, though, is protecting them from something dangerous—a possible explosion. If a bomb did explode, the bomb suit would offer protection from flying debris. More than likely, though, the force of the blast would throw the bomb tech a significant distance—maybe fifty or sixty feet. This force would cause severe bruising and per-haps even broken bones. But in many instances, the bomb suit would save the bomb tech from being killed.

A Booming Business

Most people would think that Richard L'Abbe was crazy. Or, at the very least, they wouldn't want to have his job. L'Abbe tests the eighty-pound bomb suits worn by bomb squad experts. Wearing a bomb suit, which costs about $20,000, L'Abbe stands fifteen to twenty-five feet from an explosive device. And then the bomb is detonated. As L'Abbe told *People* magazine, each time he tests the suit, it's "like getting hit by a small truck."

So why does he do it? L'Abbe is the president of Med-Eng Systems, a Canadian company that designs and manufactures bomb suits. Some bomb squad members were concerned that the suit wouldn't provide enough protection if a bomb exploded near them. "Many of them thought of bomb suits as body bags," L'Abbe told *People* magazine. So to prove that the bomb suits really will protect the bomb techs who wear them, L'Abbe exposes himself to explosions. Over the years, he has tested many bomb suits. So far, the only injuries he has received are cuts and headaches. That's good news for bomb squad members who wear bomb suits on the job!

A fully equipped bomb tech approaches a robot being used to defuse explosives on a busy street in Brooklyn, New York, during a bomb scare in March 2002.

Detonating

Disabling a bomb doesn't always mean that it must be defused. Sometimes the best option is actually to detonate it, or cause it to explode. Detonation is used only when no people are in the area. For example, bomb squad members might decide to detonate a suspicious-looking package found in a field or in the woods.

To detonate a package, a small amount of explosives is used. Although detonating a bomb can be dangerous, bomb squad experts know how to do it safely. They can control when and where the bomb goes off, making sure that no one will be near the explosion.

Containing

In some cases, explosive devices must be contained so that they can be transported. For safety reasons, bombs are usually transported in a total containment vessel (TCV). This is a large steel drum that can withstand several strong explosions. Even bombs that have already been defused are usually contained before being moved, just to be on the safe side. Bomb techs cannot afford unexpected surprises.

Bomb techs use the TCV to transport some explosive devices to a demolition range. At this isolated area, the bombs are placed in large pits dug into the land. Then they are detonated from a remote location.

Sergeant Tim Ketvirtis *(left)* and Sergeant David Vroman of the Michigan State Police Bomb Squad prepare to tow a total containment vessel along with them during a bomb emergency in Sterling Heights, Michigan. The vessel is designed to withstand a certain amount of explosive force should the bomb inside go off.

Detonating bombs is just as dangerous as the bomb itself. Explosives must be placed around the bomb carefully. The bomb itself is not tampered with. Instead, the demolition explosives are detonated around the bomb. These explosions ignite the bomb safely. When the whole package blows up, the threat is finally extinguished.

Investigating an Explosion

The bomb squad doesn't always get a chance to disarm and dispose of a bomb. In some cases, unfortunately, the bomb has already exploded before its presence could be detected. In these situations, bomb squad experts still play several vital roles.

Along with police officers, bomb techs secure the area around an explosion. In this way, they can help make sure that no one else gets hurt and that evidence is not destroyed. The bomb squad team also checks the area for additional explosives that have not yet been detonated. If any are found, they must be disarmed. And one of the bomb squad's most important roles is to find evidence that will help determine who is responsible for causing the explosion.

Major U.S. Bombings

In the past decade or so, there have been several major bombings in the United States or involving U.S. citizens. The experience and expertise of bomb squad technicians have been called upon to help solve these terrible crimes.

Pan Am Flight 103

On December 21, 1988, Pan Am Flight 103 was headed to New York from London. As the jet flew over Lockerbie, Scotland, a huge explosion blew the plane apart in midair. All 259 people on board were killed, along with 11 more people on the ground. The explosion did not take place in the United States, but many of the plane's passengers were American citizens.

Investigators needed to determine if the explosion was the result of an accident or a bomb. They immediately began combing the crash site for clues. It took nearly two years, but they found a crucial bit of evidence—a piece of a timing device used to detonate a bomb. Eventually, investigators put together the

This photo shows the devastation wrought by the crash of Pan Am Flight 103 in Lockerbie, Scotland, in 1988. Investigators were able to track down the bombing suspects using evidence smaller than a human fingernail.

pieces of the puzzle. A small but powerful bomb had been planted in a suitcase and stowed on the plane. It detonated midflight. A Libyan intelligence official was convicted of arranging the bombing.

World Trade Center

Years before the terrorist attacks of September 11, 2001, the World Trade Center in New York City was the site of a major bombing. On February 26, 1993, an explosion rocked through the parking garage below the

Emergency vehicles surround the World Trade Center after the 1993 terrorist bombing.

buildings. It was a Friday afternoon, and 50,000 people were in the 110-story skyscrapers. The blast killed six people and injured more than 1,000 others.

The New York Police Department Bomb Squad and the Federal Bureau of Investigation (FBI) were called in to investigate. The explosion destroyed six floors of the underground parking garage and created a crater that was 200 feet wide. Investigators found traces of an agricultural fertilizer, which can be used to make bombs. They determined that 1,200 pounds of explosives had been brought into the parking garage in a rental van. Once investigators found out who rented the van, they were able to make several arrests. The suspects were tried and convicted of bombing the World Trade Center. The bombing was determined to be an act of terrorism by Islamic militants.

Oklahoma City

Two years after the World Trade Center bombing, another terrorist attack struck the United States. This time, it occurred in America's heartland—Oklahoma City, Oklahoma. On April 19, 1995, a huge explosion demolished the entire front side of the nine-story Alfred P. Murrah Federal Building. When the dust settled, 168 people were dead and hundreds of others injured. At the time, it was the worst act of terrorism on American soil.

At first, many people assumed that the Oklahoma City bombing was the work of foreign terrorists.

The Oklahoma City bombing tore apart the Alfred P. Murrah Federal Building in April 1995. Bomb techs sifted through the rubble for clues as to what type of bomb was used. Here, a fireman surveys the wreckage in the parking lot.

When bomb squad experts and the FBI examined the area around the building, they found many pieces of evidence. They determined that a rented truck packed with nearly 5,000 pounds of explosives had blown up in front of the building. The truck and the explosives were linked back to Timothy McVeigh and Terry Nichols—Americans with ties to an antigovernment group. McVeigh and Nichols were both convicted of the Oklahoma

City bombing. In 2001, McVeigh was executed for his crime.

Atlanta Summer Olympics

In 1996, the Summer Olympic Games were held in Atlanta, Georgia. At this type of major event, bombs are always a potential threat. That's why bomb technicians were stationed at each Olympic venue. During the Olympics, the bomb squad experts examined many suspicious-looking packages. Most of them turned out to be harmless, but a few were destroyed just in case.

On July 27, however, bomb techs discovered the real deal. A backpack left unattended was found to contain three pipe bombs and plenty of wire. The bomb techs and police officers immediately began evacuating the area. Unfortunately, though, they could not evacuate everyone in time. The package exploded, killing one woman and injuring more than 100 other people. The bomb, armed with shrapnel in the form of six pounds of nails, was clearly intended to kill many people. Although the bomber has not yet been arrested, the FBI does have a suspect in the case.

The Unabomber

The FBI spent eighteen years searching for a terrorist who had become known as the Unabomber. Between 1978 and 1996, this criminal made sixteen bombs that killed three people and injured twenty-three others. The Unabomber often targeted people who worked for universities and airlines. He left some bombs in public places and sent others through the mail. When an unsuspecting person opened the package, it would explode.

The Unabomber was very good at covering his tracks. During his eighteen-year bombing spree, only one person got a clear look at him. A sketch based on the eyewitness's

Serial bombers like Ted Kaczynski often use the same bomb materials and construct the bombs in the same manner each time they make one.

description was added to the FBI's Most Wanted List. Because the Unabomber had been wearing a hooded sweat-shirt and sunglasses, though, investigators couldn't determine his identity.

After the longest manhunt in U.S. history, the FBI finally got the break it needed. In January 1996, a man named David Kaczynski realized that the Unabomber might be his brother, and he called the FBI. When investigators searched Theodore Kaczynski's Montana cabin, they felt that they had found the Unabomber at last. The cabin was filled with bomb-making materials, books about building bombs, and even a live bomb. Theodore Kaczynski pled guilty and was sentenced to life in prison.

Identifying a Bomber

In much the same way that many artists and writers have a recognizable style, many bomb makers also have a specific style. They often leave certain identifying marks or include signature ingredients in their bombs. For example, some bombers always make crude, homemade bombs with easy-to-find parts. Others, however, may use high-tech electronics and expensive explosives.

Bomb technicians are trained to find these types of similarities among explosive devices. This ability helps them link several bombs to one bomb maker and can often lead to the identity of the criminal. In the case of the Unabomber, for instance, the bombs' similar traits included polished wooden parts, home-made switches, and old pieces of wire.

Although identifying a bomber takes a great deal of hard work, bomb techs are sometimes helped by a little luck. In the Oklahoma City bombing, investigators had a stroke of good fortune when they found part of a truck axle among the rubble. Amazingly, the axle contained the truck's vehicle identification number (VIN), which was still readable. When investigators determined that the axle came from the truck used in the explosion, the VIN enabled them to trace the truck to a rental agency. From there, they found out who rented the truck and arrested two suspects.

The Life of a Bomb Tech

4

Bomb squad experts are a rare breed of individual. Every day, they face extremely dangerous situations. Although bomb techs are highly trained and well prepared, explosive devices are often unstable and unpredictable. Every time bomb techs encounter a bomb, they realize that many lives, including their own, are at great risk.

For these reasons, no one is forced into a career with the bomb squad. Bomb squads don't recruit their members. Even bomb techs employed by the military must volunteer for this duty. Even so, most bomb squads have many more applicants than job openings. The turnover rate tends to be low because the majority of bomb techs stay at their jobs for many years before they retire.

A Bomb Squad Career

Many bomb squad experts are employed by local law enforcement agencies, including police departments. Others work for federal government agencies, such as the FBI or the Bureau of Alcohol, Tobacco, and Firearms (ATF). The military also employs a large number of bomb technicians.

Police Departments

Small-town police departments generally don't have a need for their own bomb squad. In large cities, however, that's not the case. The more people that live in an area, the more likely that the police department will include a bomb squad. Police departments in major cities, such as New York, Chicago, and Los Angeles, have large bomb squads. Many members of police bomb squads started as regular police officers before joining the bomb squad. Some may have also been in the military.

The oldest and largest civilian bomb squad in the United States is the New York Police Department

A suspected pipe bomb brought police and bomb techs to the Roosevelt Hotel in New York City in August 2002. The bomb squad eventually removed and disposed of the bomb.

(NYPD) Bomb Squad. It has been active for more than 100 years.

Federal Government Agencies

The FBI and the ATF are the two largest federal government employers of bomb technicians. FBI and ATF bomb techs are often called in to assist local police department bomb squads. They also investigate major incidents and terrorist attacks, including the World Trade Center and Oklahoma City bombings. Most FBI and ATF bomb techs have previous experience as members of law enforcement or military bomb squads.

Military Branches

Bomb squad experts employed by the U.S. Army, Navy, or other branches of the military are called explosive ordnance disposal (EOD) technicians. Like civilian bomb techs, EOD technicians detect and disarm explosive devices. They also dispose of unexploded bombs that are occasionally found on military bases or elsewhere. Sometimes, EOD technicians are sent to foreign countries to help with clearing minefields after wars have ended.

Requirements of the Job

The work of a bomb squad expert is challenging and demanding, both physically and emotionally. A bomb threat may be called in at any time of the day or

Sergeant Kelly Roy, an air force explosive ordnance disposal technician, uses a metal detector during a search for a missing fighter jet that crashed near Vail, Colorado, in July 1997. The plane was equipped with 2,000 pounds of high-powered MK-2 bombs.

night, and bomb techs must always be prepared. They are highly trained professionals who take their jobs very seriously.

Necessary Skills

Facing a bomb that may explode at any moment can be a matter of life or death. Bomb techs must be able to handle this type of high-pressure situation on a daily basis. They need to remain calm and

Specialist Robert Hankins defuses a fake, or "dummy," bomb as a colleague watches. Bomb squad experts hone their skills by engaging in such drills.

BOMB SQUAD BIO: Dawn Smith

In the male-dominated bomb squad field, Sergeant Dawn Smith is a rarity. In 1982, Smith became the first woman to graduate from the FBI's Hazardous Devices School. She went on to become the commander of the bomb unit of the Jefferson County Police Department in Louisville, Kentucky.

When Smith was growing up in Gary, Indiana, her child-hood dream was to become a police officer. She achieved that dream when she started her first job as a patrol officer. She has also worked as an ambulance driver and an under-cover narcotics officer. Later, Smith became a sergeant in the police force and then the commander of the bomb squad.

In 1991, she was seriously injured while trying to disarm a bomb. Her injuries included damage to one eye and deafness in one ear. Even so, Smith continues to work as a member of the bomb squad, risking her own life to save the lives of others.

keep a clear head in order to do their job. Patience and nerves of steel are essential skills. A sense of fear is healthy and normal and helps bomb techs stay alert and act safely.

To locate and disarm a live bomb requires a keen eye for detail and excellent hand-eye coordination. Bomb technicians must be able to assess a situation quickly yet take the time needed to act carefully and cautiously. It is crucial that they take nothing for granted and leave nothing to chance. The bomb tech's motto is "It's a bomb until it's not a bomb."

While there are many skills that bomb squads look for in their members, there are also a few undesirable traits. For example, someone who is too anxious, easily rattled, or overly confident would not make a good bomb tech. In addition, bomb squads generally don't want to hire people who have an excessive interest in explosions.

Training and Practice

All civilian bomb technicians are trained at the FBI's Hazardous Devices School, located in Huntsville, Alabama. These bomb techs include not only those employed by the FBI and ATF but also the techs employed by police department bomb squads. At this school, trainees begin by learning basic skills, such as how to detect and disarm explosives. By the end of

A member of the Office of Law Enforcement Technology Commercialization uses a hazardous access training kit, which prepares bomb squad experts for different bomb scenarios.

the course, they have also received training in more advanced topics, including how to deal with chemical and biological weapons.

Bomb techs must keep their skills sharp and stay familiar with the latest technology. So they return periodically to the Hazardous Devices School for retraining. In addition to this training, bomb squad members continually practice disarming bombs. They build bombs that blink or set off a buzzer if they are not defused correctly. Then the bomb techs take turns testing one another to see if they can successfully defuse these practice bombs.

It's also important for bomb techs to stay up-to-date on current bombing techniques. They read books about bomb making, check Web sites about explosives, and talk to fellow bomb squad experts. This information helps bomb techs be prepared for any situation.

High-profile public events require many safety precautions. FBI bomb experts are pictured here in the press room of the 2001 Emmy Awards in Los Angeles.

The Future of the Bomb Squad

Now, more than ever, bomb squad experts are in great demand. With the recent increase in terrorism, the potential for bombings has also increased. This makes the bomb tech's skills even more invaluable in today's world.

Even as bombers create more sophisticated explosive devices, bomb squad experts figure out new ways to deal with these threats. Lieutenant Jerry Sheehan is commander of the NYPD Bomb Squad. He told the *New York Times Magazine*, "We're always working on stuff. We don't live in the past. We learn from the past. And if something new comes up, we'll handle it."

Glossary

booby trap A hidden bomb set to explode when another harmless-looking object is touched.

contain To hold a bomb in a safe vessel for transport.

defuse To remove the fuse from a bomb.

detonate To make a bomb explode.

dirty bomb Also known as an improvised radiation-dispersal device; an extremely dangerous explosive intended to spread radio-active contamination.

disarm To make a bomb harmless.

disrupter cannon A device that shoots a powerful stream of water at a bomb, disarming it before it can explode.

EOD technician Short for explosive ordnance disposal technician; a military bomb squad expert.

explosives Materials set to burst violently at a certain time.

evidence An object that furnishes proof of a crime.

hoax A bomb threat in which a weak or fake bomb is used to lure bomb squad experts into danger by exposing them to a real or more powerful bomb.

shrapnel Dangerous materials, such as nails or glass, that are attached to a bomb in order to worsen the effects of the explosion.

terrorism The use of violence to threaten or hurt people in an attempt to achieve political goals.

For More Information

Organizations

International Association of Bomb Technicians
    and Investigators
P.O. Box 16688
Arlington, VA 22215
Web site: http://www.iabti.org

World EOD Foundation
33A Church Road
Watford, Herts WD17 4PY
United Kingdom
e-mail: info@eod.org
Web site: http://www.eod.org

Web Sites

Due to the changing nature of Internet links, the Rosen Publishing Group, Inc., has developed an online list of Web sites related to the subject of this book. This site is updated regularly. Please use this link to access the list:

http://www.rosenlinks.com/ec/bose

For Further Reading

Brodie, Thomas Graham. *Bombs and Bombings: A Handbook to Detection, Disposal, and Investigation for Police and Fire Departments*. Springfield, IL: Charles C. Thomas, 1995.

Dick, Jean. *Bomb Squads and SWAT Teams*. Mankato, MN: Crestwood House, 1988.

George, Charles, and Lind George. *Bomb Detecting Dogs*. Mankato, MN: Capstone Press, 1998.

Green, Michael. *Bomb Detection Squads*. New York: RiverFront Books, 1998.

Greenberg, Keith Elliott. *Bomb Squad Officer: Expert with Explosives*. Woodbridge, CT: Blackbirch Press, 1996.

Hamilton, John, and Sue Hamilton. *Terror in the Heartland: The Oklahoma City Bombing*. Edina, MN: Abdo & Daughters, 1996.

Sherrow, Victoria. *The Oklahoma City Bombing: Terror in the Heartland.* Springfield, NJ: Enslow Publishers, 1998.

Sherrow, Victoria. *The World Trade Center Bombing: Terror in the Towers.* Springfield, NJ: Enslow Publishers, 1998.

Tomajczyk, S. F. *Bomb Squads.* Osceola, WI: MBI Publishing Company, 1999.

Bibliography

ATF Online. "Canines." Retrieved September 5, 2002 (http://www.atf.treas.gov/kids/canines.htm).

Dalton, Jacob. TechTV.com. "The Tech of: A Bomb Squad." Retrieved September 6, 2002 (http://www.techtv.com/thetechof/story/0,24330,3374727,00.html).

Green, Michael. *Bomb Detection Squads*. New York: RiverFront Books, 1998.

"Is He the Unabomber? After the Longest Manhunt Ever, the FBI Nabs a Suspect." *Time for Kids,* April 19, 1996, p. 4.

Lombardi, Kate Stone. "Busy Days for Bomb-Sniffing Dogs." *New York Times*, May 6, 2001, p. 14WC.4.

McBride, Sharon. "The Difference Between Life and Death." *Soldiers*, June 1, 2002, p. 28.

Revkin, Andrew C. "Bees Learning Smell of Bombs with Backing from Pentagon." *New York Times*, May 13, 2002, p. A10.

Schlosser, Eric. "The Bomb Squad." *Atlantic Monthly*, January 1994, pp. 23–30.

Sherrow, Victoria. *The World Trade Center Bombing: Terror in the Towers*. Springfield, NJ: Enslow Publishers, 1998.

Sullivan, Robert. "Defusing the Situation." *New York Times Magazine*, October 6, 2002, p. 36.

Tomajczyk, S. F. *Bomb Squads*. Osceola, WI: MBI Publishing Company, 1999.

Index

About the Author

Suzanne J. Murdico is a freelance writer who has authored numerous books for children and teens. She lives in Florida with her husband, Vinnie, and their cat, Zuzu.

Photo Credits

Cover, pp. 9, 12, 17, 21, 23, 25, 27, 30, 32, 35, 36, 38, 40, 45, 47, 51 © AP/Wide World Photos; p. 5 © © Howard Jacqueline/Corbis Sygma; pp. 15, 52 © Reuters NewMedia, Inc./Corbis; p. 23 (inset) © Jeffrey L. Rotman/Corbis; p. 48 © Roger Ressmeyer/Corbis.

Designer: Les Kanturek; Editor: Mark Beyer